Jesus Is the Way

INSPIRATIONAL POEMS BY A WOMAN OF GOD
ANITA BOONE

JESUS IS THE WAY

Copyright © 2018 by Anita Boone

All scripture quotations are public domain courtesy of Bible Gateway: www.biblegateway.com

All rights reserved. No part of this book may be reproduced, stored in a retrieval system, or transmitted in any form or by any means, electronic, mechanical, photocopying or otherwise without prior written permission from the author.

ISBN: 978-1-7327674-8-5

Edited by Latricia C. Bailey of LCB Enterprises

Vision to Fruition Publishing House
www.vision-fruition.com

All artwork and graphic images are property of www.pixabay.com unless otherwise cited.

ALL RIGHTS RESERVED

PRINTED IN THE U.S.A.

In Memory Of

MY FATHER: THOMAS U. TAYLOR
(UNITED STATES ARMY VETERAN, WWII)
&
MY BROTHERS:
ROY TAYLOR
(UNITED STATES ARMY VETERAN)
&
GREGORY TAYLOR
(UNITED STATES ARMY VETERAN, VIETNAM)

UNCLE ALFRED AND AUNT JUANITA AUGUSTUS (UNITED STATES ARMY VETERAN, WWII)

UNCLE WENDELL AND AUNT CASSIE DEAS

AUNT ALICE COLEMAN JACKSON

GENEVA GATLING BOONE, MOTHER-IN-LAW

In Loving Memory

THOSE WE *love* DON'T GO AWAY
THEY WALK BESIDE US EVERYDAY.
UNSEEN, UNHEARD BUT *always* NEAR
STILL LOVED, STILL MISSED AND VERY DEAR.

Dedication

I dedicate this book of poems to the Father, Son, and the Holy Spirit. For without the anointing, ***Jesus Is the Way*** would not have been written.

I dedicate this book also to my loving husband, Calvin Boone, whom I have been married to for 28 years and more to come. He has been a loving, faithful and devoted husband, father and grandfather. Thank you honey! I love you, and I thank God for bringing you into my life.

The steps of a good man are ordered by the Lord: and
he delighteth in his way
Psalm 37:23 (KJV)

I dedicate this book of poems to my Pastors/Apostles Tony and Cynthia Brazelton, my spiritual Dad and Mom. I thank God for your prayers for our marriage and family. God hears and answers prayers. May God continue to bless you and your family.

Last of all, I dedicate this book to my father, Thomas U. Taylor (deceased); and my mother, Virginia Taylor; my brother, Pastor/Apostle Thomas G. Taylor and his wife, Ruth Taylor; my mother-in-law, Geneva Gatling Boone (deceased); my two nephews, Girard and Lamone, Uncle Claude and Wendell (deceased), cousins Kevin, Bonnie, Cassandra, Roxsan, and Nathan; and, my two bonus daughters, Tonia and Stacy; and four grandkids: Princess, PJ, Alex and JR.

To my church family and all my friends and anyone who chooses to read Jesus is the Way, my prayers and hope are that they will be inspired to do great things together to make a difference in this world. May God bless all, and anyone that I have not mentioned who were instrumental in helping me throughout my life.

Christ in you, the hope of glory.
Colossians 1:27 (KJV)

Table of Contents

Foreword……………………………………………………2
Introduction…………………………………………………3
Matthew 5:1-10 (KJV) ……………………………………5
Praise the Lord!……………………………………………7
God Is Love…………………………………………………9
God Created You In His Image…………………………11
Man of God…………………………………………………13
Woman of God……………………………………………15
A Child of God……………………………………………17
He Will Never Leave You or Forsake You……………19
A Mother's Love…………………………………………21
JOY …………………………………………………………23
God Is Good ………………………………………………25
Transformed Into a Beautiful Butterfly ………………27
Winter Days ………………………………………………29
Springtime…………………………………………………31
Summer Days ……………………………………………33
Autumn……………………………………………………35
I Like Flowers……………………………………………37
This Is Your Season……………………………………39
Did You Pray the Prayer of Faith?……………………41
Taste and See ……………………………………………43
Faith ………………………………………………………45
Kindness…………………………………………………47
Patience……………………………………………………49
Believe in God for A Breakthrough……………………51
Back Down Memory Lane………………………………53

A New Day..55
Honor Mom & Dad..57
If Anyone Wants to Know..59
What Is Beauty?..61
Jesus Is the Way..63
Family Reunion...65
Joined Together as One..67
No Time to Waste..69
Jesus Is the Reason..71
Nothing Can Separate Us...73
What Can Wash You Clean?..75
Will You Be Ready?..77
Jesus is Coming Back Again..79
Train Ride to Heaven...81
Heaven!...83
Vision of Jesus..85
Vision of God's Angels..86

Foreword

Pastor Melody Adams, First Lady
New Life Church-NYC

Some books inform, others inspire. However, this book will do both. It will affirm for some and reaffirm to others that everything we will ever need in life can be found in Jesus! Therefore, I am excited, honored, and privileged to introduce, *Jesus Is the Way*, written by my friend, Anita Boone.

Anita and I met over 10 years ago as co-workers. She had over 30 years of experience and possessed a wealth of institutional knowledge that was instrumental in assisting me as a newly hired Supervisor at the Agency. Beyond Anita's professional skills and abilities, is her meek and gentle spirit. She is a woman of love, integrity, impeccable ethics, reliable, humble, consistent, and compassionate. No matter what tests, trials, or tribulations that would surface at work, I loved that Anita always remained calm.

Anita exemplifies the Proverbs 31 virtuous woman! She lives her life grounded in the Word, and the love she and her husband, Calvin share towards one another, is admirable. When you see them together, they resemble two teenagers who are happy and immensely in love with each other. They have fun and both share a love for God and tennis! They are beautiful to watch and model an example of what God intended marriage to be.

In this book, you will find many attributes that speak to this phenomenal woman, Anita Boone. I am so proud of her for sharing *Jesus Is the Way*, A Collection of Inspirational Poems, full of dreams and visions of love for all to enjoy! She is a believer/Christian sharing her overflow of love. She is a gift to the body of Christ. May you be blessed by reading this book and be reminded and reaffirmed that, "*Jesus is the way, the truth and the life.*" John 14:6-7 KJV

Introduction

Jesus Is the Way is based on inspirational poems, my life experiences, stories, testimonies, spiritual truths, and revelations received from God. I received Christ Jesus as my personal Lord and Savior at the age of twelve years old. My passion for writing poems did not begin until 1978 when a news editor asked me to write a poem on *Summer Days*.

One of my favorite Biblical stories is the Sermon on the Mount. According to Matthew 5:1-10, Jesus saw the crowds and went up on a mountainside and sat down. His disciples came to him and he began to teach on the Beatitudes. He promised a reward for each one of those that diligently sought him. Jesus made clear that he did not come to abolish the Law or the Prophets but to fulfill them according to Matthew 5:17. His teaching was to show his disciples and people how to be righteous and to love and forgive one another. Jesus further teaches them how to pray to God by giving them the *Lord's Prayer* according to (Matthew 6:5-13). These same teachings are used in our daily walk with Christ today.

The title of my book, *Jesus Is the Way,* came to me when I understood how Jesus made a way for us through his death on the cross for the redemption of our sins so that we can receive salvation and eternal life. According to John 3:16, *"For God so loved the world, that he gave his only begotten Son, that whosoever believeth in him should not perish, but have everlasting life."* The Bible tells us that Jesus is the one and only way to God who is our main source. According to John 14:6, *"Jesus saith I'm the way, the truth, and the life: no man cometh unto the Father, but by me."*

No matter what our position or title is in life, all of us have fallen short. According to Romans 3:23, *"For all have sinned, and come short of the glory of God."* Therefore, we must confess of our sins according to Romans 10:9-10: *"That if thou shalt confess with thy mouth the Lord Jesus, and shalt believe in thine heart that God hath raised him from the dead, thou shalt be saved. For with the heart man believeth unto righteousness; and with the mouth confession is made unto salvation."*

I hope that you will enjoy reading my poems of inspiration and pray that they will be a blessing into your life.

Matthew 5:1-10 (KJV)

Image by Robert Cheaib from Pixabay

1 And seeing the multitudes, he went up into a mountain: and when he was set, his disciples came unto him:

2 And he opened his mouth, and taught them, saying,

³ Blessed are the poor in spirit: for theirs is the kingdom of heaven.

⁴ Blessed are they that mourn: for they shall be comforted.

⁵ Blessed are the meek: for they shall inherit the earth.

⁶ Blessed are they which do hunger and thirst after righteousness: for they shall be filled.

⁷ Blessed are the merciful: for they shall obtain mercy.

⁸ Blessed are the pure in heart: for they shall see God.

⁹ Blessed are the peacemakers: for they shall be called the children of God.

¹⁰ Blessed are they which are persecuted for righteousness' sake: for theirs is the kingdom of heaven. Matthew 5:1-10 (KJV)

Praise the Lord!

Image by Clker-Free-Vector-Images from Pixabay

Praise the Lord!

Let us go into the house of the Lord to praise and worship our King!
Make a joyful noise as you enter into his Holy Gates and sing!

Sing songs of joy and of his great love,
and give him thanks for his blessings from above.

He is our strength and hope for tomorrow,
and he gives us peace in times of sorrow.

He is worthy to be praised for his mercy and grace.
He gives us the victory to win in this race.

Oh, bless his Holy name, our Lord reigns!
Let all the earth give him Honor and Glory as our King of Kings, He remains!

Let everything that hath breath praise the Lord. Praise ye the Lord.
Psalm 150:6 (KJV)

God Is Love

Image by John Hain from Pixabay

God Is Love

God is love, and he cares for you.
His love is genuine and true.

He desires for us to live and be free,
and has prepared a place for you and me.

His love reaches out to the depths of the sea,
and is present for the whole world to see.

God created us in his image and likeness.
His love is good and filled with kindness.

God loved us so much, he gave his only Son, Jesus—Who
died for our sins on the cross to save us.

Give thanks to God for his love every day.
Open your heart to receive his love
as you go along the way.

Give thanks to the Lord, for he is good. His love endures forever.
Psalm 136:1 (NIV)

God Created You in His Image

Image by LoveToTakePhotos from Pixabay

God Created You in His Image

God separated the light from the darkness,
and he created you in his image and likeness.
He placed the sun, moon, and stars in the sky;
Then he blessed us and opened our spiritual eye.

Now, we must do all that he called us to be,
Living and walking in perfect harmony;
Giving each other hope for tomorrow;
Peace and joy in times of sorrow.

Each of us are special and unique in his sight,
and God watches over us day and night.
We must lift our eyes to the Lord,
and trust and obey his holy word.

And no matter where we are in life today,
God is on our side each day.
All we must do is call on Jesus,
and he will always answer us.

To God Be the Glory!

So God created man in his own image, in the image of God created he him; male and female created he them. Genesis 1:27(KJV)

Man of God

Man of God

Man of God, you are called by God today,
as a spiritual leader, to follow God in every way.

You go forth with love and joy each day,
and you always take time to pray.

You give others hope to face tomorrow,
and you encourage those in time of sorrow.

You show others that you really do care,
Not only about yourself, but in helping those in despair.

Always remember to thank God every day.
Praise him for his goodness and love as you go along the way.

Believe in God, for he is a kind and compassionate friend;
And know that he is with you, even until the end.

He will answer you when you call,
and pick you up, if you should stumble or fall.

But thou, O man of God, flee these things; and follow after righteousness, godliness, faith, love, patience, meekness.
1 Timothy 6:11 (KJV)

Woman of God

Image by waldryano from Pixabay

Woman of God

Woman of God, you are a daughter of the most-high King;
Rise and shine, and go forth before the Lord, and sing!

You are chosen for this time and generation;
One who honors God and will go before the nation.

You always watch as well as pray,
And you submit your will to doing the work of the Holy Spirit each day.

Wait on the Lord and always listen to his voice.
Follow his words, and he will help you make the right choice.

You are a precious jewel in God's sight,
and a bright shining light!

You are an example for others to follow,
Giving them hope for tomorrow.

Take heed to his teachings and obey;
and always give thanks to God every day.

She openeth her mouth with wisdom; and in her tongue is the law of kindness. Proverbs 31:26 (KJV)

A Child of God

A Child of God

I am a child of God of the most-High King!
Jesus lives in me and will always reign.

I am blessed from my heavenly father above.
He fills me with his presence and love.

I thank God for my earthly parents each day;
and ask the Lord to bless them when I pray.

I need them to help guide me to follow God's Holy word,
and to encourage me to listen and to obey the Lord.

I am a child of God and each day that I grow,
My hopes and dreams are for a better tomorrow.

I will always trust and obey him every day,
Because I want to enter the gates of Heaven someday.

Train up a child in the way they should go: and when he is old, he will not depart from it. Proverbs 22:6 (KJV)

He Will Never Leave nor Forsake You

Image by StockSnap from Pixabay

He Will Never Leave Nor Forsake You

You are the apple of God's eye
and the light that shines in darkness beneath the sky.

God loves you just the way you are
and cares for you, no matter how near or far.

He promised to never leave nor forsake you,
and he will do just what he said He will do

Never look back at your past,
But always look forward to your future, and hold fast.

Life is precious, so live each day,
and always remember to give God thanks and pray.

And, lo, I am with you alway, even unto the end of the world. Amen.
Matthew 28:20 (KJV)

A Mother's Love

Image by OpenClipart-Vectors from Pixabay

A Mother's Love

A Mother's love is one that cares for you.
She will wrap her arms around you and make you feel brand new.

She will pick you up when you don't have a friend around,
Or help you if you stumble or fall down.

She is a warm and gentle soul sent from heaven above,
and will give you peace and much love.

She listens and obeys the Lord,
and is someone who trusts in his word.

She prays for God to watch over her family day and night,
to keep them in his marvelous light.

But we were gentle among you, even as a nurse cherisheth her children. 1 Thessalonians 2:7 (KJV)

JOY

Joy

Have joy when you wake up each day
before you do anything!
Always give thanks to God when you pray.

Sing a song or have laughter with one another,
Lifting spirits and love for your sister or brother;
Trust in God in times of sorrow,
Knowing that he will take care of tomorrow.

Let us give the joy of Christ to all we meet!
Give them hope, when we go out to greet.

Encourage them with a kind word or two,
and tell them Jesus died for me and you,
When you wake up each day in the morning
before you do anything.

To God Be the Glory!

O come, let us sing unto the Lord: let us make a joyful noise to the rock of our salvation. Let us come before his presence with thanksgiving, and make a joyful noise unto him with psalms.
Psalm 95:1-2 (KJV)

God Is Good

God is good, and he is good all the time.
He is my bright and morning sunshine.

He is a loving and compassionate friend,
and he is always with us until the end.

His divine Holy Spirit and presence is everywhere;
and why you should know that he cares.

He will take care of you every day;
and he always hears you when you pray.

God desires the best for you and me,
and he wants us to be prosperous and free.

Let us praise his holy name, for he is worthy
of all praise!
And his goodness and mercy shall follow us
for the rest of our days.

Christ in you the hope of glory!
Colossians 1:27 (KJV)

Transformed Into A Beautiful Butterfly

Image by Oldiefan from Pixabay

Transformed Into A Beautiful Butterfly

You were just a caterpillar, then you changed
into a beautiful butterfly one day.
You started out slow but came a long way.
With my eyes all aglow, you were lovely to see,
and your colors were bright as can be.

You were attractive in your orange, black, and white.
I wanted to catch you by your wings in flight,
and then hold you in my hand;
But you took off somewhere else to land.

You were like a sunbeam of hope and love,
A tiny creation sent from heaven above.
I'll always remember you as my little butterfly,
But most of all, how you made it look so easy to fly.

And be not conformed to this world: but be ye transformed by the renewing of your mind, that ye may prove what is that good, and acceptable, and perfect, will of God.
Romans 12:2 (KJV)

Winter Days

Image by Couleur from Pixabay

Winter Days

Gone already are those days filled with snow,
When yet we had but a few more days to go.

Watching the sun rise into the pure blue skies,
Melting the snow piles right before my eyes.

And while it had slowly begun to drift away,
Signs of springtime were soon to come this way

With lots of cherry blossoms just waiting to appear,
Making it seem as though winter days were never really here.

While the earth remaineth, seedtime and harvest, and cold and heat, and summer and winter, and day and night shall not cease. Genesis 8:22 (KJV)

Springtime

Image by Jill Wellington from Pixabay

Springtime

What a beautiful time of the year to enjoy the sun;
Go out for a walk in the park, or go for a run;

A time to feel the warmth of each day,
and to see the birds fly away;

A good time to see the flowers in the morning,
Or listen to the gospel music and sing;

Enjoy cooking on the grill,
Or going to a movie and chill.

A time to thank God for waking us up to see,
And enjoy another day to be free.

It's a happy time to spend with family and friends;
Sharing our hopes and dreams, and precious memories and all good things.

See! The winter is past; the rains are over and gone. Flowers appear on the earth; the season of singing has come, the cooing of doves is heard in our land. Song of Songs 2:11-12 (NIV)

Summer Days

Image by Steve Bidmead from Pixabay

Summer Days

I like summer days for the blue skies and
sunshine so bright.

I like summer days for the beautiful flowers
are such a warm delight.

I like summer days for the butterflies
on my finger alight.

But, most of all, I like summer days to hear the sounds of
crickets at night,

And lightning bugs that sparkle by the moonlight.

*Every good and perfect gift is from above, coming down from the
Father of the heavenly lights, who does not change like shifting
shadows. James 1:17 (NIV)*

Autumn

Image by Adam Derewecki from Pixabay

Autumn

Open your eyes, the fields are already white.
There is an abundant harvest in sight.

Let us go out into the fields and bring in the harvest,
Giving thanks to God for he gives us his best.

Then, let us go out to tell others about Jesus,
and how God loved us so much, he sent his only Son
to die on the cross for us.

Be sure to tell them they can be saved and set free,
and live to enjoy life more abundantly.

God will open doors for everyone,
and for us to come together in Christ as one.

It's harvest time!

Say not ye, There are yet four months, and then cometh harvest? behold, I say unto you, Lift up your eyes, and look on the fields; for they are white already to harvest. John 4:35 (KJV)

I Like Flowers

I Like Flowers

I like flowers so radiantly bright.
Mums come in a variety of colors to delight.
It brings me a sense of joy and admiration,
for its beauty and artful decoration.

Lilies bring me peace deep within,
and it's like the breath of Spring.
Sunflowers are yellow and like the sun,
Makes me laugh and have some fun!

While roses make me feel love, which
is good for my emotion,
Giving me time for my devotion,
Orchid flowers are so lovely to see,
and their beauty is exotic to me.

But most of all, daisies make me cheerful,
and appreciate how flowers can be so beautiful.
They make me even more thankful for the smaller things,
while cherishing our family and friends.

*And why take ye thought for raiment? Consider the lilies of the field,
how they grow, they toil not neither do they spin.
Matthew 6:28 (KJV)*

This Is Your Season

Image by OpenClipart-Vectors from Pixabay

This Is Your Season

The moment you always waited for is finally here.
We wish you all the best of happiness and good cheer!

We thank you for all your contributions throughout the year, knowing that there is something else in store for you.
Because you are such a beautiful person and so true.

We will not forget all your years of service and dedication;
Your work and loyalty were truly an inspiration.
We will keep you in our prayers each day, and always remember,
Your retirement from this place on this 17th day of December.

Yes, this is your season, and it is yours to always treasure.
Always keep the faith, and do the things you like beyond measure.

Live each day to the fullest and reach for the stars above,
And know your heavenly Father sends you all his love.

To God Be the Glory!

Ms. Jordan,

We wish you success and much happiness!

Did You Pray the Prayer of Faith Today?

Image by Vickie McCarty from Pixabay

Did You Pray the Prayer of Faith Today?

Did you pray the prayer of faith today?
He will surely answer you in his time
and in his own way.

All you must do is ask God and believe,
and open your heart to receive.

And if you pray the prayer of faith to the Father,
He will forgive you like no other.

So, if you have not stopped to pray,
Then now is the time today.

You can pray the prayer of faith to the Lord,
and thank him, for he always keeps his word.

And the prayer of faith shall save the sick, and the Lord shall raise him up; and if he has committed sins, they shall be forgiven him.
James 5:15 (KJV)

Taste and See

Taste and See

Taste and see the goodness of the Lord.
Take heed and listen to his Word.

His Word is sweeter than the taste of wine,
and is holy and divine.

It is sharper than any two-edged sword,
and our faith is strengthened in the Lord.

His love is far better than money can buy,
Blessing you each day from on high.

Study his word, and you will see,
God's power of love and mercy.

O, taste and see the goodness of the Lord.is good: blessed is the man that trusteth in him. Psalm 34:8 (KJV)

Faith

Image by Dan Fador from Pixabay

Faith

Faith is trusting in God no matter what others may say,
and keeping the faith is why we pray.

Your faith gives you hope for tomorrow;
Peace, love and joy in times of sorrow.

With faith you can do all things through Christ who strengthens you,
Knowing that God will make all your dreams come true.

You can say to that mountain, "Be thy removed!"
And by having and keeping the faith, how can you lose?

All you need is faith the size of a tiny mustard seed.
It will give you the power to speak and succeed.

Just know that you must keep the faith and believe,
Then open your heart to receive.

If ye have faith as a grain of mustard seed, ye shall say unto this mountain, Remove hence to yonder place, and it shall remove, and nothing shall be impossible unto you. Matthew 17:20 (KJV)

Kindness

Image by rawpixel from Pixabay

Kindness

When you are kind and gentle to one another,
You are showing the love of God for your brother.

This will help brighten up their day
and encourage them along the way.

Give someone a smile or say a kind word or two.
When you do this, God will bless you.

Spending time together is more precious than anything.
It means all the world and is everything.

Do to others as you would have them do to you.
Luke 6:31 (NIV)

Patience

Patience

Everyone must learn patience, especially when
we are put to a test.
If you find yourself in a hurry, you must slow
down at best.

Then wait on the Lord, and he will strengthen you.
He will guide you through and make things new;
and give you courage in times of trouble,
so that you will not fall or stumble

With patience, you don't have to worry or get upset,
or be angry, because you'll soon forget.
Because being patient is a part of growing up.
It helps you face tomorrow no matter what.

*Be anxious for nothing, but in everything, by prayer and supplication
with thanksgiving let your requests be made known unto God.
Philippians 4:6 (NKJV)*

Believe In God
For A Breakthrough

Image by Patrick Neufelder from Pixabay

Believe In God For A Breakthrough

Believe in God for a breakthrough.
He will make all your dreams come true.

He will pick you up and turn you around,
and plant your feet on solid ground.

He will give you courage and hope to face tomorrow,
and peace and joy in times of sorrow.

There is nobody greater than the Lord,
and he always keeps his word.

All you must do is trust and obey;
Believe in God, and he will answer you when you pray.

Ask, and it shall be given you; seek, and ye, shall find; knock, and it shall be opened unto you: Matthew 7:7-8 (KJV)

Back Down Memory Lane

Image by Abby Haukongo from Pixabay

Back Down Memory Lane

Days, months and years have passed and gone by,
when prices for a loaf of bread weren't so high.

I remember when you could buy ice cream,
and Dreamsicles from the truck;
or buy a bag of candy for less than a buck.

It was a time to remember the fun games that we used to
play with our friends.
Hopscotch, Double Dutch, Mother May I?, Tree Tag, and
Red-light were just a few of our favorite things.

But no matter how many games we used to play,
When it was time to go to church on Sunday,
Our parents made sure this was part of our day.

And even though, we didn't have a cell phone,
Jesus was always with us, and we never felt alone.

When I was a child, I spoke as a child, I understood as a child, I thought as a child but when I became a man, I put away childish things. 1 Corinthians 13:11 (KJV)

A New Day

Image by Rujhan Basir from Pixabay

A New Day

While I have lived throughout this land,
I've learned how to take a stand.

I have walked up many roads, you see.
Without God on my side, where would I be?

He put food on my table and a smile on my face.
He healed my body and put me in a better place.

He is a giver and wants the best for us each day.
And I will rejoice in him and continue to pray.

His presence is inside of my heart.
He makes me feel happy, and we will never part.

I will always praise his Holy name,
Because he has changed my life, and
I'll never be the same.

Therefore, if any man be in Christ, He is a new creature, behold, old things have passed away and all things are become new.
2 Corinthians 5:17 (KJV)

Honor Mom & Dad

Image by OpenClipart-Vectors from Pixabay

Honor Mom & Dad

When we obey our parents, God will bless us,
and you will see the love of Jesus.

God wants us to honor our Mom and Dad.
It helps us in life to be happy when we're sad.

When we receive God's love, peace, and happiness,
He will bless us to have health, prosperity,
and good success.

And when we trust and obey his words of love,
He will grant us favor and blessings from above.

We are important to him, and he wants us to know
by honoring our parents is the way to go.

So, always listen to your Mom and Dad each day,
and ask God for guidance when you pray.

*Honor your father and your mother, so that your days may be long
upon the land which the Lord your God is giving you.
Exodus 20:12 (NKJV)*

If Anyone Wants to Know

If Anyone Wants to Know

If anyone wants to know why your faith is so strong,
or what makes you know right from wrong;
And if anyone wants to know why you can hear from the Lord, then tell them:
"It's made possible, because Jesus' Word is my sword."

If anyone wants to know why you praise God in song,
or wants to know how you can endure for so long.
And if anyone wants to know why you pray,
Then tell them Jesus loves me and I will obey.

If anyone wants to know why people talk about you,
or wants to know why you are loyal and true.
And if anyone wants to know why you believe,
Then tell them:
"Christ died for our sins, and all we must do is open our hearts to receive."

To God Be the Glory!

My sheep hear my voice, and I know them, and they follow me.
John 10:27-28 (NKJV)

What Is Beauty?

Image by StockSnap from Pixabay

What Is Beauty?

Beauty can be attractive and lovely to see.
But what do I think beauty means to me?

Another person may not feel the same way.
It is in the eyes of the beholder anyway.

But true beauty radiates from the heart inside,
and blossoms like a flower on the outside.

It is someone who is gentle and kind,
and speaks blessings with others in mind.

And beauty does not come from what we wear
or the color of our skin or hair.

But what pleases God is that we show his
beauty everywhere.

Your beauty should not come from outward adornment, such as elaborate hairstyles and the wearing of gold jewelry or fine clothes. Rather, it should be that of your inner self, the unfading beauty of a gentle and quiet spirit, which is of great worth in God's eyesight. 1 Peter 3:3-4 (NIV)

Jesus is the Way

Image by Rama Krishna Karumanchi from Pixabay

Jesus Is the Way

When you don't know what to do
or which way to go, because you're feeling blue;
When life seems unfair and too hard,
and you quit moving forward;
Then look up to Jesus and pray,
and he will take all your troubles away.
He will pick you up and turn your life around,
and plant your feet on solid ground.
You don't have to reach for a bottle of alcohol or wine,
because God's love is heavenly and divine;
and he will forgive you of all your sins today.
Only believe in God and that
Jesus is the way.

Jesus saith unto him, I am the way, the truth, and the life: no man cometh unto the Father, but by me. John 14:6 (KJV)

Family Reunion

Image by mohamed Hassan from Pixabay

Family Reunion

This is a time for us to always remember;
when we celebrate our family reunion together,
and enjoy God's blessings for us to treasure,
Filling our hearts beyond good measure.

It is a very special time of the year to behold,
Lots of good times and memories to hold.
Surely, this is a dream come true,
And time to see what God has for me and you.

God hears and answers our prayers every day.
And we give thanks to our Father when we pray.
He is worthy of all praise and knows everything,
and God is good and a reason for us to sing.

A family that prays together, stays together

Joined Together as One

Image by mohamed Hassan from Pixabay

Story of How I Met My Husband, Calvin

I prayed to God that the Lord would send me someone that would someday become my husband. I asked God for a man who was God-fearing, and one that would love me for who I am. I asked for someone who was nice and enjoyed being together with me.

Then on Saturday morning, on September 30, 1990, I got up and went to the bathroom to wash my face. While rinsing my face, the Holy Spirit spoke to me and said, "You may meet someone today." Before I could finish drying my face, he told me again two more times, "It's a possibility that you may meet someone today."

Well, later that morning, I went to have some work done on my car at Goodyear's located on Silver Hill Road. It was so busy, the salesperson said to me, "Why don't you get yourself some breakfast?" So, I did. I went up the street to McDonald's and ordered my breakfast from the drive in. Instead of driving off, I decided to eat my food in the car. Little did I know that I would meet my future husband, Calvin, who was already parked right next to me. He got my attention and asked me to give him the time. He introduced himself to me, and this is how we met. Later, he explained that he had also prayed to God to meet someone. He almost went to play tennis, but at the last minute he decided to go to McDonald's for breakfast. I was glad that we were both obedient and listened to God.

To God Be the Glory!

No Time To Waste

No Time To Waste

God gives us 365 days a year,
And the time is drawing near.

We must go forward and don't look back.
Start picking up the pieces and stay on track.

He woke you up to see a new day,
and he started you on your way.

It's because of his love, mercy, and grace,
You are still in this human race.

So, don't give up and don't you quit.
There is no time to waste because you're it!

So, teach us to number our days that we may apply our hearts unto wisdom. Psalm 90:12 (KJV)

Jesus Is the Reason

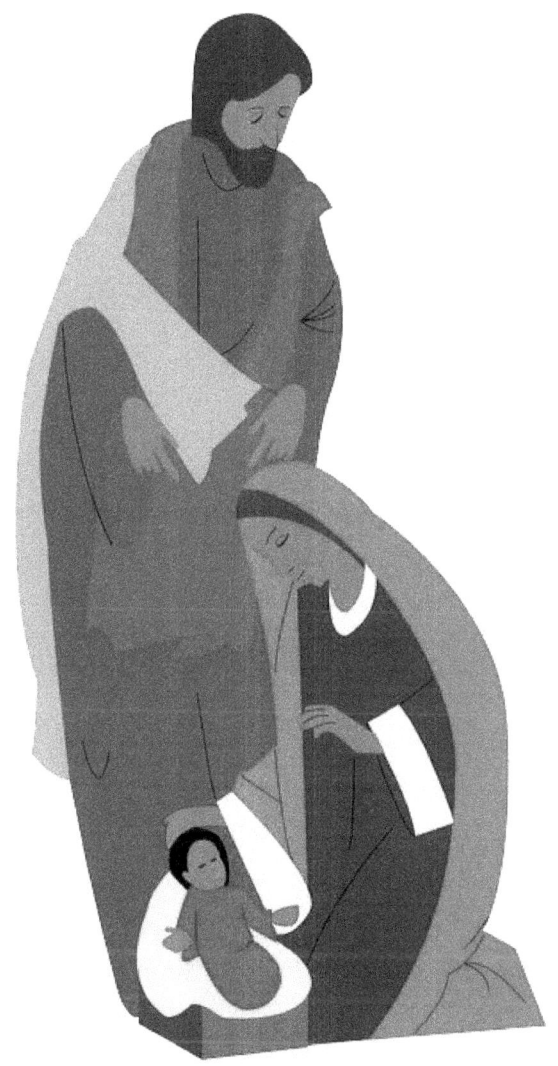

Image by Clker-Free-Vector-Images from Pixabay

Jesus Is the Reason

God is our father in Heaven above.
He is merciful and full of love.

He sent the Holy Spirit upon us all,
and is always ready to hear us when we call.

Let us spend Christmas time this year
With our family and friends who are dear.

Showing our love for one another and
Not forgetting our sisters and brothers.

When we celebrate the Lord's birthday
in December,
Always remember, Jesus is the reason
for the season!

> *For unto us a child is born, unto us a son is given, and the government shall be upon his shoulder: and his name shall be called Wonderful, Counsellor, The mighty God, the everlasting Father, the Prince of Peace. Isaiah 9:6-7 (KJV)*

Nothing Can Separate Us

Image by Jeff Jacobs from Pixabay

Nothing Can Separate Us

As deep or wide as the Pacific Ocean,
and as long as the Amazon River,
As far as the north is to the south,
and the east is to the west;
No valley on earth or mountain,
or sun, moon or stars;
Not even the planet Venus
will or can separate us.

Nothing can separate us from God's love
and his mercy from above.
He was in the beginning,
and will be in the end.
He is our Father who art in heaven,
and his love will endure forever!

To God Be the Glory!

For I am persuaded, that neither death, nor life, nor angels, nor principalities, nor power, nor things present, nor things to come. Nor height nor depth, nor any other creature, shall be able to separate us from the love of God, which is in Christ Jesus our Lord.
Romans 8:37-39 (KJV)

What Can Wash You Clean?

Image by Jeff Jacobs from Pixabay

What Can Wash You Clean?

Soap and water can wash away the dirt from your skin every day;
But it will never wash away the hurt or your sins away.

The only thing that can wash you as white as snow
Is nothing but the blood of Jesus, don't you know?

He will never leave you or forsake you,
and his words are true

All you have to do is call on his name,
and you will find your life will change.

But if we walk in the light, as He is the light, we have fellowship one with another, and the blood of Jesus Christ His Son cleanseth us from all sin. 1 John 1:7 (KJV)

Will You Be Ready?

Image by Gerd Altmann from Pixabay

Will You Be Ready?

The doors of the church are open to one and all.
Listen and obey when you hear your master's call.

Like Paul on his way to Damascus at war,
No doubt, God had another plan for him in store.

When he fell from his horse, he saw a bright light.
Then a wonderful change came over him overnight.

Truly, God sent His only begotten son, Jesus.
He died on that old rugged cross for us.

We must not be like those in the days of Noah,
and miss out;
Because Jesus will come back again with
a loud shout!

Yet, no one knows the hour or day.
Will you be ready if the trumpet should sound today?

As it was in the days of Noah, so it will be at the coming of the Son of Man. Matthew 24:37 (NIV)

Jesus Is Coming Back Again

Image by Gerd Altmann from Pixabay

Jesus Is Coming Back Again

When Jesus was born of a virgin,
The whole world was living in sin.

God sent His only begotten son Jesus
So we could have everlasting life.

He went out to feed the hungry and teach,
and He would go out daily to preach;
Heal the lame to walk, the blind to see,
and to set the captives free.

Death could not hold him down.
He arose and ascended into heaven,
and He fulfilled his mission on the earth.
But one day, Jesus is coming back again!

Behold, he cometh with clouds, and every eye shall see him, and they also which pierced him; and all kindreds of the earth shall wail because of him. Even so, Amen.
Revelation 1:7 (KJV)

Train Ride to Heaven

Train Ride to Heaven

There is a train going out non-stop to Heaven,
and it's scheduled to leave on gate seven.

Get on board all of God's children! Don't be late,
and miss out not going through the gate.

Leave all your cares and your troubles behind.
Where you're going, you will have a peace of mind.

No more crying and no more dying,
but rejoicing and life everlasting.

So, get your one-way ticket, there's no turning back.
Be ready to get off at the next stop.

All aboard, next stop is to a Holy place in the sky above;
A place filled with all of God's holy angels and his love.

To God Be the Glory!

And suddenly there was with the angel a multitude of the heavenly host praising God and saying, "Glory to God in the highest, and on earth peace, good will toward men.
Luke 2:13-14 (KJV)

Heaven!

Heaven

Heaven is a place we will find
filled with joy and so much love,
Unspeakable joy and peace of mind;
A place so bright, it must shine!

A place where the angels behold
the beauty of God's Holy face,
shining radiantly as pure gold,
a very special place.

A place to worship our Creator,
the Almighty God and King;
Where we dress in white to adore,
and give thanks and sing.

A place where the waters run,
and there is a tree of life.
No more need for the sun,
and no more misery or strife.

A place where there is no more crying
and no more dying,
and there will be no more sorrow
or worry for tomorrow.

*And I saw a new heaven and a new earth: for the first heaven and
the first earth were passed away; and there was no more sea.
Revelation 21:1 (KJV)*

Vision of Jesus

At the early age of six years old, I always would try to envision how Jesus looked. There were pictures of the *Lord's Last Supper* and other paintings of him around the house. Then one day, while resting on the sofa in the living room before going to school, I fell asleep, and Jesus appeared to me in a vision. He was dressed in a blue and white cloak and was sitting on a rock surrounded by a body of blue water. Before awakening from my sleep, I was touched by the hand of Jesus. The room was filled with the presence of the Holy Spirit all around me, and all I could remember was jumping up on my feet to see him with my natural eyes, but the Holy Spirit kept my eyes closed. I stumbled over the coffee table, and I made my way upstairs one step at a time until I reached the top of the stairs. My eyes opened, and I ran quickly down the hall way to tell my older brother. I went on to school that day and I was filled with so much joy and peace. I knew then that God had something special for me in my life.

Vision of God's Angels

Image by Pete Linforth from Pixabay

In the summer of August 1989, before waking up, I had a vision of four angels that appeared dressed in white and a rainbow in the background. The first one did not have any wings and appeared shorter, but the other three angels had wings. All the four angels stood facing upward like they were on stairs to Heaven. I remember asking one of the angels if it was male or female, and it responded that it was neither one or the other. I prayed to God to reveal to me what could this mean. When I went out to work that day I felt God's love and presence, a sense of joy and peace, and a desire to be closer to God. I felt a sense of energy, healing, protection and became more inquisitive about the four angels dressed in white with wings.

I read how God's archangels and angels are messengers from God. They protect and guide us and carry out other heavenly tasks. The color white and wings indicate purity, peace, blessings, and rejuvenation. Then I started researching the Bible for more information, and I found in the book of Revelation 7:1-4, how the four angels were standing on the four winds of the earth, so that the wind should not blow on the earth, nor on the sea, nor on any tree. And God had given them charge to do no harm to the earth, neither the sea, nor the trees until we have sealed the servants of our God in their foreheads. Also, I found in the book of Revelation 4:3, that the rainbow was round about God's throne in sight like unto an emerald. The rainbow represents God's protection for his people and is like the times of Noah during the flood upon the earth. He separated Noah and his family from the rest of the humans and the flood did not hurt them (Genesis 7:1). Likewise, God desires to seal the hundred and forty and four thousand tribes of the children of Israel.

    I began to pray to God that all my family and friends would be saved and all those desiring to enter the kingdom of God would be in that number.

    To God Be the Glory!

Testimony:

On August 25, 2011, I went to work, and it was business as usual. Then around 11:30 am, I was going to take a rather early lunch, but for some reason I felt inclined to go back to work. Before I could go back into the building, I could feel earth tremors underneath my feet. For a moment, it felt like the earthquake was going to cause the building to collapse. I could hear the building shift where I worked. I ran over to some of the other ladies standing on the corner of Virginia Avenue NW, Washington, DC. I was able to run over to them and say a prayer together with them. I asked God to dispatch his angels over the earthquake immediately in the mighty name of Jesus, Amen! In less than a minute, I felt a peace and calmness I never had before, and I felt the presence of the Holy Spirit and his love around us.

The next day, my husband and I were getting ready to go to work and he asked me if I was going to Bible study that night. I remembered telling my husband, "No, I plan to stay home, especially after what happened yesterday." Then I noticed the door from our bedroom slightly move by itself as if the Lord was waiting to see what I was going to do. So, I told my husband that I changed my mind. I will be going to Bible study tonight. Upon leaving church that evening, I received a text message from one of our neighbors informing us of an 'Emergency', and for us to come home quickly. Little did my husband and I know that our house was on fire and we wouldn't be able to go back inside. This fire started from our neighbor's house, spread over to our house and went over to another one of our neighbor's home. The damage was so severe and devastating that we were not allowed to go back inside of our house.

My husband and I had to relocate the same night of the fire. The Red Cross placed us in a hotel for three nights. Later on, the insurance company moved us into another place, but God blessed us to find a nice place within the area within walking distance to the metro station while our townhouse was being renovated. After waiting for eight months, we went out looking at some new single-family houses, and God blessed us to find one in January 2012. In the meantime, we had a close family friend who recommended us to a real estate agent. She along with her co-worker helped us to sell our townhouse in District Heights, Maryland. By May 2012, our townhouse sold exactly one year later from the time our townhouse caught on fire. We thanked God for our friends and prayers.

The effectual fervent prayer of a righteous man availeth much.
James 5:16 (KJV)

Testimony:

One day while driving on Silver Hill road in District Heights, Maryland after work, I noticed a man begging on the side of the street. My husband was with me that day, so I decided to give the man some money in his cup. The man was very thankful and told us if we ever need anything, he would return the favor. Well, it wasn't too long after that I drove down the same street, and my car stopped in the left lane. I thought one of the passersby in a vehicle was going to stop to help, but they just kept going. A police officer saw me, and he kept on going too. Then I looked up and saw the same man that I had given some money to offering me his help. He literally pushed my car across the street to the old Shakey's Pizza place, so I could call for help. I went to call for roadside assistance and went back outside the restaurant. The man was nowhere in sight. I thought he must have been an angel in disguise.

Journal

Journal

A Tribute to my father Thomas Ulysses Taylor
April 14, 1921 – December 5, 2003

A ceremony was held on May 29, 2004 by the National Monument in honor of all of those that served their country during World War II. My father's name is on the list of names and it was a privilege to attend the ceremony to celebrate the thousands of veterans of the war and 16 million Americans who served in the armed forces during World War II and the men and women killed in the fight against Germany, Italy and Japan.

     My father was a devoted father, husband, and grandfather who loved his family. He was born in the District of Columbia and had one sister. He was a faithful member of Liberty Baptist Church since 1930. He served as a Jr. Trustee for many years and became a member of the Sr. Usher Board. He was good at drawing sketches and painting, playing the piano, and enjoyed listening to Christian music. He was married to my mother, Virginia Taylor, for over 61 years. My father retired from working at the Department of Veteran's Affairs after 41 years of service and received various commendations, awards and certificates.

Thomas Ulysses Taylor served in the United States Army from 1943 to 1945. On November 3, 1943, the U.S.A. was at war with Germany and Japan. My father was a truck driver with the 476th Amphibian Truck Company stationed in Florida, Georgia, Louisiana, and Seattle Washington. April 7, 1945, known as D-day, my father was wounded on the Amphibian DUKW "Duck Boat" ship when the Japanese were firing at his team's airplanes. The fighting happened on the Island of Iwo Jima. Some of the shells were hitting the Duck Boat causing shrapnel to penetrate both of his legs, making him fall off the Duck Boat into the Pacific Ocean.

Back at home, the family had received a telegram from the United States Department of War that he was missing-in-action. By the grace of God, my father swam back towards the purple beach shore until a naval patrol boat came and rescued him and brought him back to his outfit. A newspaper reporter, Ernie Taylor Pyle, had interviewed him about being thrown into the ocean. My father later received a telegram from the Red Cross that his mother was ill. On November 13, 1945, he was given an honorable discharge from the Army and was released to go home to be reunited with his family.

My father, Thomas Ulysses Taylor, was the recipient of a Purple Heart, two bronze medals, the Good Conduct Medal, National Heart Medal, a Combat Medal, American Theater Service Ribbon, Asiatic Pacific Theater Service Ribbon and World War II Victory Ribbon.

A Tribute to My Brother, Gregory Allen Taylor
November 16, 1946 – February 1, 2011

My brother was a loving, kind and giving person. He was the youngest of the three brothers. We would always play together and walk home from school. He attended Providence Baptist Church and went to Sunday school along with us at Kentucky Avenue, S.E., Washington, DC. He was baptized at the Free Gospel Church, Coral Hills, Maryland in 1993. Gregory enjoyed playing baseball and watching the Washington Redskins play football.

On November 8, 1965, at an early age, Gregory volunteered to join the United States Army as an Intelligence Specialist in the 1st Cavalry Armored Division. He served his country, and received a Purple Heart, the National Defense Service Medal, Vietnam Service Medal, two bronze service stars, and Republic of Vietnam Campaign Ribbon with a device and sharpshooter badge with rifle bar. Gregory was honorably discharged after being wounded in Vietnam and returned home on November 15, 1968.

On January 3, 2006, Gregory was united to the love of his life, Betty. He was a loving and devoted husband who touched so many lives. He became an active member at the Christian Fellowship Trumpet Outreach Ministries in 1994, our brother, Pastor/Apostle, Thomas Taylor's church. We thank God that he received the Lord Jesus as his personal savior before he transitioned to be with the Lord.

A Tribute to My Brother Roy Ulysses Taylor
May 26, 1943 – October 31, 2009

My oldest brother was a loving father of five children. He was baptized at Providence Baptist Church formerly located on Kentucky Avenue Southeast in Washington, DC. Later, he became a member of the Free Gospel Church, Coral Hills, Maryland. He was talented in drawing sketches and knew how to do Hieroglyphic Writings. He was mechanically inclined and worked on cars. He was always dressed sharp in his cadet uniform at Eastern High School and was good at running track.

He served in the United States Army when he was eighteen years old for three years during the Cuban Crisis. He was stationed in Fort Carson, Colorado, and went to Florida to be on standby in case of an attack. In April 1965, he received an honorable discharge. He worked as a Chef at Bolling Air Force Base and later worked as a civilian at Andrews Air Force Base and served as one of the head Chefs for the Captains and Generals. Everyone loved Roy for his baritone voice, humor and laughter. Later, he became an active member at the Christian Fellowship Trumpet Outreach Ministries in 1995 under the pastoral leadership of our brother, Pastor/Apostle, Thomas G. Taylor.

We thank God that he received the Lord Jesus as his personal savior before he transitioned to be with the Lord.

A Tribute to My Aunt "Sis"
Juanita G. Taylor Augustus
August 9, 1923 – August 16, 1991

Aunt Sis was a devoted wife, mother and grandmother. She loved her family and was a Woman of God. Sis was a faithful member of the Albright Methodist church in Washington, DC and received her education in the D.C. Public School System. Upon graduation from Armstrong Senior High School, she enrolled at Howard University. She interrupted her college career to serve in the United States Army from January 1945 to September 1946. She returned to Howard University and obtained a Bachelor of Science degree in Physical Education. She moved to Bermuda to teach physical education in the school system. While in Bermuda, she met and married Alfred A. Augustus. They returned to the United States to live and she completed her master's degree at Columbia University in New York City.

Aunt Sis taught in the D.C. Public School System for over 30 years. She was a dedicated educator and imparted a love of knowledge to each of her students. Her love of children and teaching carried over into her church life at Albright. She taught Sunday school and Vacation Bible School for 25 years and shared her love for the Lord with each of her Sunday school children. She received the Teacher of the Year Award while teaching at Nannie Helen Burroughs Elementary School in the District of Columbia.

A Tribute to my Uncle "Curly"
Nathan Adams, Sr.
June 26, 1931 – March 25, 2018

Nathan Adams Sr. was a loving husband, father and grandfather. He was born the second youngest of 7 brothers and a sister. Nicknamed because his hair was always, you guessed it, Curly, he was also known for his love of working with his hands. He served as a Marine during the time of the Korean War and was wounded. He was the recipient of a Purple Heart.

Curly enjoyed doing carpentry work and could always be found in his workshop crafting a bookcase, entertainment unit, tables, shelves, and more. If it could be made from wood, he could fashion it. His easy smile and friendly "hello" was known throughout the block, where all anyone had to do was to stand outside of the house and wait to be greeted. Sooner or later he would appear. He enjoyed spending time working on the garden in the backyard, hedging the bushes, or adding touch-up paint where needed. He always made sure that the cabinets were stocked full of food and could be counted on to be a gracious host when entertaining. He also loved to have cook-outs, where his hamburgers were most famous. Any given Saturday the backyard would be chock-full of teenagers playing board games, often Monopoly marathon sessions lasting over 2 days.

Acknowledgements

I want to take this time to thank my God for blessing our marriage and for healing me and keeping my family. I give him all the praise, all the glory, all the honor and inspiration for being able to write my poems, *Jesus is The Way*. I thank my Pastors/Apostles Tony and Cynthia Brazelton for being such good role models for me to follow. I also thank them for praying for our family.

To my husband, Calvin, I thank you for being a devoted husband, father, grandfather, and a man of God. We have been married for more than 28 years of marriage, and you have been truly a blessing to me. Your prayers and support for the family and the body of Christ will always be remembered and deeply appreciated. Therefore I'm dedicating my book to God and you.

To my Mom and Dad (deceased), I thank you both for raising me up and for teaching me the word of God and the importance of going to church and how to make something out of my life. To my brother, Pastor/Apostle Thomas Taylor and his wife, Ruth, and family and friends, I thank you all for your love and support.

To my former supervisors, Pastor Melody Adams, John and Minister Terry, I would like to thank you all for your support throughout my career. You were always there as an inspiration and would give me good advice. I would like to also thank my former pastor, Reverend Pointer from Providence Baptist Church, Minister Vernell and Ministers John and Claire for their prayers and support. I would like to thank Debra, Nanette, Sarah, Cecelia and all of my former co-workers in the Information and Programs and Services (IPS).

To my good friends Sharon and Dave, I would also like to thank you all so much for your love and support. Special thanks to Jane (deceased) and Carolyn for their support and helping us to sell our townhouse in Forestville, MD.

To the Deacon Ministry, Fishers of Men (FOM), and Children's Church, and Virtuous Women Ministry, much love to all of you. I would like to especially thank Minister Kesha, for recommending Minister LaKesha Williams of Vision to Fruition Publishing, for her help in bringing to a completion this book, in Jesus' name, Amen.

May God bless all my family and friends and anyone that I have not mentioned who were instrumental in helping me throughout my life.

To God Be the Glory!

About the Author

Lois Anita Taylor was born to Thomas Ulysses and Virginia Louise Taylor in the District of Columbia in 1950 at Georgetown Hospital. Her family refers to her as Lois, but she goes by Anita.

To know Anita is to experience her loving, patient and warm spirit. She has a passion for working with the homeless, elderly, and serving her community. Anita is a Deacon at Victory Christian Ministries International (VCMI). She also enjoys serving as an Altar Lead.

Anita is a faithful wife, mother of two bonus daughters, Tonia and Stacy and four grandchildren: Princess, PJ, Alex, and J.R. She has been married to Calvin Boone for twenty-eight years. And currently resides in Southern Maryland and her work history includes working at the United States Department of State as Management Analyst in Records Management and Program Analyst. Her last place of employment was working in the Department as a Lead Program Analyst/Government Information Specialist for the Freedom of Information Act and Privacy Act programs in the Office of Management and Public Diplomacy (MPD). Upon occasion, she would serve as Acting Branch Chief. She has also worked at other federal agencies throughout her career. After 43 years of United States Government service, she retired and received the Expeditionary Service Global Award, the United States flag and the Secretary's Career Achievement Award in 2016.

Anita graduated from Eastern High School with honors and received a BA degree in Political Science and minor in Sociology from Dunbarton College of Holy Cross in 1973. She also attended Trinity College majoring in Special Education. She worked as a school teacher for the Young, Gifted, and Talented. Her favorite color is royal blue. She attended many of the Virtuous Women's Conferences at the Victory Christian International Ministries (VCMI) church and is a member of the Fishers of Men (FOM).

Anita enjoys reading, watching tennis and religious movies and listening to gospel music. One of her favorite songs is *"I Never Knew Love Like This Before"*, *"He's Intentional"*, *"Center of My Joy"* and *"Break every Chain"*. Her favorite Christian movie is *"Jesus of Nazareth."*

About the Publisher

At **Vision to Fruition Publishing**, we are dedicated to helping others bring their personal, business, ministry & nonprofit visions to fruition.

Whether it's as grand as a book you want to write, a business you want to start, a conference or event you want to host, a ministry you want to launch or an organization you want to start; or as small as needing a computer repair, logo design or web design; **Vision to Fruition Publishing** will help you walk through the process and set you up for success! At **Vision to Fruition** we don't have clients, we have Visionaries. We provide solutions to equip others to pursue their visions & dreams with reckless abandon.

In 2018 we published twenty-three authors, eight of which were Amazon Bestsellers. We would love for you to join our family of Visionaries as well!!!

Learn more here: www.vision-fruition.com

www.ingramcontent.com/pod-product-compliance
Lightning Source LLC
Chambersburg PA
CBHW071148090426
42736CB00012B/2273